Foundations to Truth

I0622983

by

Dawei

B180 Basketball, Inc.
P.O. Box 2406
Midland, MI 48641-2406
www.b180basketball.com

Published by B180 Basketball, Inc. 2-16-24

ISBN: (sc) 979-8-9913306-0-2
ISBN: (e) 978-1-7325361-9-7

Library of Congress Control Number:

2024916760

Contents

Dedication

This book is dedicated to all living individuals in the world. Continue to seek grow and give.

Acknowledgments

I would like to acknowledge and thank God (of Abraham, Isaac, and Jacob), the Holy Spirit, Jesus Christ (Son of God), and my parents.   Thank you and I love you always.

Introduction

To become wise, a person must learn to ignore the world and seek himself. As time passes by man begins to ponder and grow from each sorrow. This causes man to seek the unknown. The unknown becomes truth as man finds God and is opened to life. God affirms that each human being is a reflection of God. God, Spirit, and man creates tomorrow.

This book will help an individual search within themselves for answers to life's problems. In this book are messages of spiritual guidance and nourishment. This book will help individuals to:

- Discover your current view of the world

- Discover your inner self

- Learn to grow and give

- Find a source of happiness within

Note:

The views in this book are the author's views. For additional information on personal growth and development you can get information and resources from your health and wellness providers.

Chapter 1

Chapter 1

Tear Drops to Heaven

The best that a human gives is seen by God.

Worldly happenings and messages sent are logged

The heart of the human is constantly tempted.

When the water clears, God's hand holds the

commands that were mentioned.

A voice heard, a cry given, and a spirit delivered

builds the foundation to truth.

Belief opens the foundation of youth.

Continuously man walks through the world blinded

by pain.

Holding on to God's commands makes mankind

grow, concur, and love again.

Chapter 2

Chapter 2

Challenge of the Human

Caught in a world of temptation, deceit, and pain; the human seeks a hidden promise.

As man hurts man, the spirit cries and hurts while leaving half of the commands as love is missed.

Temptations defeats man as man attempts to discover.

Communication unanswered leaves the soul to ponder.

Life creates as the human builds.

The commands and love of God strengthens the human will.

Chapter 3

Chapter 3

Overcoming

Day after day the struggles exist.

Change after change the promise seems missed.

Before the heart gives, it must deny its ways.

The bridge was built to better man and nurture the days.

Leaving all that is seen challenges the human.

To build the spirit, the human must give all love to the new man.

Hand in hand God, Spirit, and Man creates.

Following the commands opens the door as God dictates.

To overcome the habit, man builds as well as destroys.

Ultimately man must give the heart of man with everlasting joy.

Chapter 4

Chapter 4

Ecstasy

Imagination has no limits.

The hand of God touches man as they create.

Access to truth is granted as love is given to those who wait.

Day after day, night after night, the passion within man grows to kiss tomorrow.

Truth exposes man to life as God carries man through each sorrow.

To use the human for gain limits the human and his seed.

Ecstasy exists when man meets spirit and walks with God.

Love is given unconditional to man, spirit, God, and those in need.

Chapter 5

Chapter 5

A Cry From Above

Each day is created by God.

The promise of what was created builds paradise.

To love when there is no love shares truth.

Happiness is found when man cries and seeks.

The hand of God is touched and nurtures the meek.

The promise is given as man grows, gives, and molds.

A cry from above gives spirit to man when the soul is sold.

Chapter 6

Chapter 6

A Golden Token

As love learns from the past, the spirit of God enters
with a gift that will ever last and build the man to
seek truth.

Truth unfolds life as a changed life delivers proof.

Belief of the mother within takes the spirit and
nurtures the world.

The love within is set free to seek and open the doors
to tomorrow.

Give life to where there is no life.

Give love to where there is no love.

Touch the heart of a stranger and deliver the promise
from above.

Continuously seek all that was spoken.

The friend within will leave life a golden token.

Chapter 7

Chapter 7

Beauty

Remembering the vision opens the heart.

The web of love keeps spirit and man apart.

The eyes of God fills truth to the world.

To nurture what's within nurtures spirit, man, boy,

and girl.

Vision after vision and thought after thought recreates

the passion that was left.

Beauty unfolds truth in man and all that is felt.

When lonely, beauty yearns and hurts.

As spirit and man unite the beauty that's seen

emerges.

Touched from above the human is blessed.

As man meets spirit the soul begins to rest.

Chapter 8

Chapter 8

Deepest Wish

I wept last night. The world deserves more.

The physical gain and monetary profit hinders pure love.

Can man leave himself?

Can a life be built?

Overtaken by truth man and spirit meet to create.

The God of Abraham, Lord of Armies gives commands and opens life to life.

Faith in truth has no crime.

The human nature of the being is planned to control time.

Step into love and deliver the promise.

When love is given by spirit tomorrow is granted by the deepest wish.

Chapter 9

Chapter 9

Everlasting

Open the door to love and experience the heavenly gift.

The promise within is released at the right time to the right human, and in the right setting.

Hopes and wishes bow to truth when love walks freely across the earth.

Deceit and temptations are defeated by the word.

The power within develops the human.

The human seeks and gives birth to love.

The promise is released as God leaves an everlasting kiss.

Chapter 10

Chapter 10

The River

God of Abraham's gift flows through the just human.

Freely love enters the lowly man.

The temple of love is seen and built by man as the

spirit is united.

The strength of man walks to truth as man overcomes

that which was blighted.

Walk after walk man meets spirit.

When time gives spirit life man must give.

Temptations brings tears of the past to light that the

spirit doesn't know.

The seeking man gives the spirit to the soul and

grows.

The dream and vision within man creates the river

that gives love as God and God begins to open doors

that builds only roads that he knows.

Chapter 11

Chapter 11

Better Than Sex

The love of God fulfills the being with truth.

Born to deliver the being becomes living proof.

Together it must be as it was written.

Faith determines love and all that is given.

Conquer truth, conquer tomorrow as God gives love.

Rescued from sorrow man gives love that's sent from above.

Filled with truth love is not denied.

The man that gathers is humbled as man uncovers what's delivered as lies.

The bottom of truth is clear and dry.

Sex without love gives the seeker a hollow cry.

Being to being sex gives life without measure.

The gift from God becomes the ultimate treasure.

Chapter 12

Chapter 12

Truth

To feel the truth and let it live opens life.

Turn back from false love and drink from the
everlasting fountain of love.

All pure, all giving, and all love, truth seeks the
seeker and delivers the unseen.

To build hope on the initial thoughts from the self,
causes man to weep.

The fall of man prepares the chambers of the soul to
build strength to give.

Rain nurtures the soul and opens the spirit within to
live.

Chapter 13

Bonus

Directions:

Write down your goals for the next 12 months.
Use the guide that follows to help you seek
truth.

Month: January

Use the space below on this page to write five (5) goals for the month and then draw a picture of yourself accomplishing the goals.

Write down 5 goals that you want to accomplish in the month.

Goals:

1.
2.
3.
4.
5.

Draw a picture below of you accomplishing <u>at least one</u> (1) of your five goals.

Picture:

Month: February

Use the space below on this page to write five (5) goals for the month and then draw a picture of yourself accomplishing the goals.

Write down 5 goals that you want to accomplish in the month.

Goals:

1.
2.
3.
4.
5.

Draw a picture below of you accomplishing <u>at least one</u> (1) of your five goals.

Picture:

Month: March

Use the space below on this page to write five (5) goals for the month and then draw a picture of yourself accomplishing the goals.

Write down 5 goals that you want to accomplish in the month.

Goals:

1.
2.
3.
4.
5.

Draw a picture below of you accomplishing <u>at least one</u> (1) of your five goals.

Picture:

Month: April

Use the space below on this page to write five (5) goals for the month and then draw a picture of yourself accomplishing the goals.

Write down 5 goals that you want to accomplish in the month.

Goals:

1.

2.

3.

4.

5.

Draw a picture below of you accomplishing <u>at least one</u> (1) of your five goals.

Picture:

Month: May

Use the space below on this page to write five (5) goals for the month and then draw a picture of yourself accomplishing the goals.

Write down 5 goals that you want to accomplish in the month.

Goals:

1.
2.
3.
4.
5.

Draw a picture below of you accomplishing <u>at least one</u> (1) of your five goals.

Picture:

Month: June

Use the space below on this page to write five (5) goals for the month and then draw a picture of yourself accomplishing the goals.

Write down 5 goals that you want to accomplish in the month.

Goals:

1.

2.

3.

4.

5.

Draw a picture below of you accomplishing <u>at least one</u> (1) of your five goals.

Picture:

Month: July

Use the space below on this page to write five (5) goals for the month and then draw a picture of yourself accomplishing the goals.

Write down 5 goals that you want to accomplish in the month.

Goals:

1.

2.

3.

4.

5.

Draw a picture below of you accomplishing <u>at least one</u> (1) of your five goals.

Picture:

Month: August

Use the space below on this page to write five (5) goals for the month and then draw a picture of yourself accomplishing the goals.

Write down 5 goals that you want to accomplish in the month.

Goals:

1.

2.

3.

4.

5.

Draw a picture below of you accomplishing <u>at least one</u> (1) of your five goals.

Picture:

Month: September

Use the space below on this page to write five (5) goals for the month and then draw a picture of yourself accomplishing the goals.

Write down 5 goals that you want to accomplish in the month.

Goals:

1.
2.
3.
4.
5.

Draw a picture below of you accomplishing <u>at least one</u> (1) of your five goals.

Picture:

Month: October

Use the space below on this page to write five (5) goals for the month and then draw a picture of yourself accomplishing the goals.

Write down 5 goals that you want to accomplish in the month.

Goals:

1.
2.
3.
4.
5.

Draw a picture below of you accomplishing <u>at least one</u> (1) of your five goals.

Picture:

Month: November

Use the space below on this page to write five (5) goals for the month and then draw a picture of yourself accomplishing the goals.

Write down 5 goals that you want to accomplish in the month.

Goals:

1.
2.
3.
4.
5.

Draw a picture below of you accomplishing <u>at least one</u> (1) of your five goals.

Picture:

Month: December

Use the space below on this page to write five (5) goals for the month and then draw a picture of yourself accomplishing the goals.

Write down 5 goals that you want to accomplish in the month.

Goals:

1.
2.
3.
4.
5.

Draw a picture below of you accomplishing <u>at least one</u> (1) of your five goals.

Picture: